KV-638-527

To read fluently is one of the basic aims of anyone learning English as a foreign language. **And it's never too early to start**. Ladybird Graded Readers are interesting but simple stories designed to encourage children between the ages of 6 and 10 to read with pleasure.

Reading is an excellent way of reinforcing language already acquired, as well as broadening a child's vocabulary. Ladybird Graded Readers use a limited number of grammatical structures and a carefully controlled vocabulary, but where the story demands it, a small number of words outside the basic vocabulary are introduced. In *Heidi* the following words are outside the basic vocabulary for this grade:

cards, ghost, goat, hay, loft, miss (verb), wonderful

Further details of the structures and vocabulary used at each grade can be found in the Ladybird Graded Readers *leaflet.*

A list of books in the series can be found on the back cover.

British Library Cataloguing in Publication Data

Ullstein, Sue
    Heidi.
    I. Title   II. Willey, Lynne
    III. Spyri, Johanna, *1829-1901*. Heidi
    428.6'4
    ISBN 0-7214-1212-0

First edition

Published by Ladybird Books Ltd Loughborough Leicestershire UK
Ladybird Books Inc Auburn Maine 04210 USA

Printed in England

Heidi

written by Sue Ullstein
illustrated by Lynne Willey

Ladybird Books

Heidi lives with her Aunt Dete.
Her mother and father are dead.

One day Aunt Dete says, ''Come
with me, Heidi. We are going
up the mountain.''

They walk and walk. They meet
one of Aunt Dete's friends.

"Where are you going?"
the friend asks.

"We're going up the mountain,"
Aunt Dete says. "We're going
to see Heidi's grandfather.
Heidi's going to live with him."

"But he's an old man,"
Aunt Dete's friend says.
"Heidi can't live with him."

"She must," Aunt Dete says.
"I'm going to work in the big
city. Heidi can't come with me."

Heidi and Aunt Dete walk on.
They see a boy with some goats.
His name is Peter. He is taking
the goats up the mountain.
Heidi walks with him to her
grandfather's house.

Grandfather comes
out of the house.

Aunt Dete says, ''This is Heidi.
She's going to live with you.
I'm going to work in the big city.
Goodbye.''

Then she goes away down the
mountain. Peter takes
grandfather's goats. He goes on
up the mountain.

"Can I go into your house, Grandpa? I want to see my new home. Where must I sleep?" Heidi asks.

"I don't know," her grandfather says.

Heidi goes up into the loft under the roof. There is a lot of hay in the loft.

"Oh, please can I sleep here?" Heidi asks. "I can make a bed in the hay. It's beautiful here."

"Yes, you can sleep here," her grandfather says.

Grandfather gives Heidi some
goat's milk. Then she goes to
bed in the loft. She looks out
of the window. She can see the
mountains and the stars.

The next day Peter comes again.

"Where are you going with the goats?" Heidi asks.

"I'm taking them to the top of the mountain," Peter says.
"The grass there is good in the summer. Do you want to come with me?"

"Yes, please," Heidi says.
"Can I go, Grandpa?"

"Yes," her grandfather says.
The two children go up
the mountain with the goats.

Heidi has a wonderful day on the
mountain. She plays with Peter
and the goats. She likes the
trees and the flowers. "This
mountain is beautiful," she says.

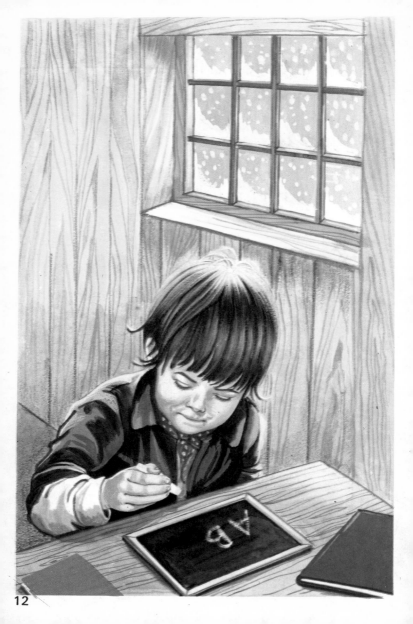

Every day Heidi goes to the
top of the mountain with Peter
and the goats. She is very
happy in her new home.

But winter comes. Snow falls
and the goats cannot go up
the mountain. Peter goes
to school in the village.
Sometimes he comes to see
Heidi after school.

One day he says, "Please come
to my house, Heidi. My
grandmother wants to meet you."

"Oh, please can I go now?"
Heidi asks her grandfather.

But her grandfather says,
"No, Heidi, not today. But
I'll take you tomorrow."

The next day Grandfather says,
"Come with me, Heidi. Let's go
to see Peter's grandmother."

Heidi is very happy. They go
down the mountain to the village.

At Peter's house Grandfather
says, "Go in, Heidi. I'll
come back soon."

Heidi goes into the house.
Peter's grandmother cannot see.

"Who is it?" she asks.

"It's me, Heidi," Heidi says.

Peter's grandmother is very happy.
She and Heidi talk and talk.
Soon Heidi's grandfather comes
back.

"I'll come back soon," Heidi says
to Peter's grandmother. "Goodbye."

One day Aunt Dete comes to see
Heidi and her grandfather.
"Heidi must come with me now,"
she says. "I want to take her to
the big city. There is a sick girl in
the city. She needs a friend. Her
mother is dead and her father is
often away. He wants Heidi to
live with them in the big city."

"Go away," Heidi's grandfather says. He is very angry. "Heidi is happy here with me."

"No," Aunt Dete says. "Heidi is a big girl now. She must go to school. Come with me, Heidi."

"No," Heidi says. "I'm happy here. I don't want to go to the big city."

"You must come," Aunt Dete says.

Heidi is sad.

"Can I come back home soon?"
Heidi asks.

"Yes, yes," Aunt Dete says.
"But we must go now."

Aunt Dete takes Heidi to the big city. They go to the sick girl's house. Then Aunt Dete goes away.

The girl's name is Clara. She cannot walk. She sits in a chair all day. She is happy to see Heidi. But Clara's teacher does not like Heidi.

"This child from the mountains isn't a good friend for Clara," she thinks. "Clara needs a city friend."

The teacher begins to tell Heidi about the city. But Heidi is very tired. She goes to sleep in her chair!

The next day Heidi looks out
of the window. There are streets
and houses, but there are no trees
or flowers or mountains.

"I don't like the big city,"
Heidi thinks. "I want to go
home to the mountains."

In the morning Heidi and Clara do some school work.

In the afternoon Heidi tells Clara about her home in the mountains. She tells her about her grandfather, Peter, Peter's grandmother and the goats. Clara likes Heidi.

One day Clara's grandmother
comes to the house. She likes
Heidi. Heidi likes Clara and
her grandmother but she does not
like Clara's teacher. And she
does not like the big city.
She wants to go home. She
misses her grandfather and
the mountains. Every night she
dreams about her home in
the mountains.

One night the teacher hears a noise. She sees a white thing. Is it a ghost?

26

Clara's father is away. The teacher sends him a letter.

"You must come home," she says. "There's a ghost in the house."

Clara's father comes home. He
does not go to bed. He sits
with his friend. His friend is
a doctor. They want to see
the ghost. They play cards and
talk. Then they hear a noise.
They see a white thing. Is it
a ghost? No, it is Heidi!

"This is our ghost!" they say.
"What are you doing here?"

"I don't know," Heidi says.

"Come with me, Heidi," the
doctor says. "I'll take you
back to bed."

The doctor takes Heidi back to bed. "What did you dream about?" he asks.

"I dreamt about my grandfather and Peter and Peter's grandmother."

"Were you very happy in the mountains?" the doctor asks.

"Yes, I was," Heidi says.

"Aren't you happy here?"
the doctor asks.

"I mustn't say that," Heidi
says. "They are very kind to
me here."

"Yes," the doctor says. "Now
you must go to sleep, Heidi.
I'll talk to Clara's father
about you. I can help you."

The doctor talks to Clara's
father about Heidi.
"Heidi isn't happy here,"
he says. "She misses her
grandfather and her home in the
mountains. She must go home."

Heidi is happy, but Clara
is sad.

"Can't Heidi stay here with me?"
Clara asks her father.

"No, she can't," her father says.
"She must go home now. But
you can go and see her soon."

Clara's teacher takes Heidi
back to the village in the
mountains. Heidi goes to Peter's
house. Peter's grandmother is
very happy.

Then Heidi goes on up the
mountain.

Grandfather sees Heidi.

''Heidi, Heidi,'' he says. ''My little Heidi. I'm very happy.''

"Hello, Grandpa," Heidi says.
"I'm very happy. They were
kind to me in the big city,
but I missed you very much."

Soon Peter comes down the
mountain with the goats. He is
happy, too. He and Heidi talk
and talk. Heidi tells him about
the big city. Then Peter goes
home.

Heidi has some goat's milk.
Then she goes to bed in
the hay loft under the roof.
She does not walk in her sleep
here. She is happy again.

Every day Heidi goes to the
top of the mountain with Peter
and the goats. Then one day
Heidi gets a letter. The
letter is from Clara. Clara
and her grandmother are coming
to see Heidi.

Heidi does not go up the mountain
with Peter. She stays at home.
She is waiting for her friends.

Heidi waits and waits. Then
she sees some men. They are
carrying Clara up the mountain.
Clara's grandmother is there,
too. Heidi is very happy.
They talk and talk.

Heidi's grandfather asks Clara,
"Do you want to stay here
with us?"

"Yes, please," Clara says.
"Can I stay, Grandma?"

"Yes, you can," Clara's
grandmother says. "I'll come
back for you in a few days."

That night the two girls sleep
in the hay loft. They are
very happy.

The next day Peter comes to
get the goats.
"Let's go up the mountain,
Heidi," he says.

"I can't come with you today,"
Heidi says. "My friend Clara
is here. She can't walk."

Peter goes on up the mountain.
He is sad. He wants to be
with Heidi.

One day Heidi says, "Grandpa,
can we carry Clara up to the
top of the mountain? It's so
beautiful up there."

"Yes," her grandfather says.
"We can carry her in her chair."

The next day Peter comes to get
the goats. Clara's chair is
near the house. Suddenly it
goes away down the mountain.
Peter tries to catch it, but
he cannot.

Peter goes on up the mountain.

Soon Heidi comes to get the
chair. She cannot find it.
Heidi and her grandfather
look and look for it.

"I'll carry Clara up the
mountain," Grandfather says.

Heidi and Clara are happy on the mountain with Peter and the goats. Heidi goes to look at the flowers.

"Clara must see the flowers over there," Heidi says. "But she can't walk. Help me, Peter. Let's carry Clara."

Peter and Heidi try to carry Clara, but they cannot. Then Clara puts her feet on the grass. She tries and tries.

"Look! Look! I can walk!" she shouts.

Heidi and Peter watch her.
They are very happy.

Grandfather comes to get Clara.

"Look! Clara can walk,"
Heidi says.

Every day Clara walks more and
more. Then she writes a letter
to her grandmother. The letter
does not say, "I can walk."
But it says, "Can you come to
Heidi's house, Grandma?"

Clara's grandmother comes to
the house. She stops at the door —
she sees Clara! Clara is walking!

"Hello, Grandma," Clara says.
"Look! I can walk. Heidi and
Peter have helped me."

"This is wonderful!" Clara's
grandmother says. "Your
father will be very happy."

Clara and Heidi look down the
mountain. They see a man.

''It's Daddy!'' Clara shouts.

The two girls run to meet him.

''Is this my little Clara?''
her father asks.

"Yes, it is," Clara says.
"I can walk and run now!"

"This is wonderful!" Clara's
father says. "I'm very happy."

"We are all happy," Heidi's
grandfather says.

49

Peter comes down the mountain with the goats.

"Is that Peter?" Clara's grandmother asks.

"Yes, it is," Grandfather says.

"Hello, Peter. You are a good, kind boy. You have helped Clara to walk. We must thank you. We are all very happy," Clara's grandmother says.

"Yes, thank you very much, Peter," Clara's father says.

"Now I want to meet your grandmother, Peter. Will you take us to her, please?" Clara's grandmother says.

"Yes, I will," Peter says.
"She wants to meet you, too.
She'll be very happy."

And she was.